WHAT 'AM SAYIN' TO YOU IS...

A BIOGRAPHY OF MALCOLM DINGWALL MACKAY

BY DAVE AND ALAN STEWART

Copyright © 2024 by Daval Publishing Ltd

All rights reserved.

No portion of this book may be reproduced or transmitted in any form or by any means without written permission from the publisher.

Contents

Dedication	1
Acknowledgements	2
Foreword	4
Preface	5
1. 'Out O' The East There Came A Big Man'...	7
2. 5, 4, 3, 2, 1	18
3. When Harry met Malky	32
4. The Wanderer(s)	42
5. 'The First Cut is the Deepest'	53
6. The Palaces	62
7. 'Extra Time'	79
8. '...To See Oursels As Ithers See Us'	89
About the Authors	106

FOREWORD

ALEX FERGUSON

...ing back all those years to my time at Queen's Park, ...alky Mackay was a young player there and was ...ith the youth team. As the records show, his history ...'s Park produced well over 300 appearances as a ...d he also proudly represented his country 20 times ...teur.

...siasm for Queen's Park was easily recognised and his ...ve for his club was unmistakeable. After a fantastic ...reer he was honoured to be installed as President of ...ark, a fitting tribute to a true Queen's Park legend ...d man.

This book is dedicated to

Malky, his Family and 'The Beautiful Game'

Acknowledgements

An army of people came to our aid in the writing of this book. None was a conscript – everyone involved freely volunteered their services. When each person was invited to contribute, two things happened. Number one – a huge smile appeared on their face and, number two, they enquired – 'How can I help?' Such was their enthusiasm and eagerness to be a part of the story. Without the contributions and efforts of all those involved, this book would have remained but a dream.

The co-authors offer their sincere thanks and appreciation to:

Derek Allan, advisor; **Tam Brodie**, friend; **Richie Brown**, Darwin Creative Media; **Peter Buchanan**, QPFC; **Kirstie Couzens**, Castle Vale Publishers Ltd; **Sean Davenport**, QPFC; **Zoe Diompy**, ACF Sports Promotions Ltd; **Matt Edwards**, friend; **Graeme Elliot**, J C Roxburgh (Insurance Brokers) Ltd; **Sir Alex Ferguson**; **Niall Harding**, West Coast Traincare Ltd; **Jim Hastie**, QPFC;

PREFACE

At 17 years old I (co-author Dave) have survived three weeks working in my first job in an engineering insurance company in Glasgow City Centre.

Payday is now forty-eight hours away; in the office I note I am the youngest. There are some interesting characters, particularly a big guy whom everyone just calls 'Malky'.

It is now Thursday lunchtime and I am planning yet another cheese roll and a saunter round the town but, hold on, Malky appears with a "Get your coat on young fella' – you're coming to lunch with us."

Moments later I am walking down St Vincent Street with him and one other, both of us struggling to keep up with him.

A voice booms out from the other side of the road – "Malky, how are you big man?"

Without slowing Malky shouts back "Champion thanks Billy, good to see you."

I glance at the other pavement. There stands Billy McNeill, the captain of Glasgow Celtic, the captain of Scotland and the first British man to lift the European Cup. A man whose stature and commanding style earned him several nicknames, the best one we think being 'Caesar'.

And he knows Malky!

After relating this story to co-author Alan (Dave's brother), Alan said "There must be a good tale to tell here."

So, more than fifty years later, what follows is the story of Malcolm Dingwall Mackay and his contribution to and his love for football.

It is a life based on service to the game of football and is predicated on the Club motto 'Ludere Causa Ludendi' or in other words, 'to play for the sake of playing'.

PREFACE

At 17 years old I (co-author Dave) have survived three weeks working in my first job in an engineering insurance company in Glasgow City Centre.

Payday is now forty-eight hours away; in the office I note I am the youngest. There are some interesting characters, particularly a big guy whom everyone just calls 'Malky'.

It is now Thursday lunchtime and I am planning yet another cheese roll and a saunter round the town but, hold on, Malky appears with a "Get your coat on young fella' – you're coming to lunch with us."

Moments later I am walking down St Vincent Street with him and one other, both of us struggling to keep up with him.

A voice booms out from the other side of the road – "Malky, how are you big man?"

Without slowing Malky shouts back "Champion thanks Billy, good to see you."

I glance at the other pavement. There stands Billy McNeill, the captain of Glasgow Celtic, the captain of Scotland and the first British man to lift the European Cup. A man whose stature and commanding style earned him several nicknames, the best one we think being 'Caesar'.

And he knows Malky!

After relating this story to co-author Alan (Dave's brother), Alan said "There must be a good tale to tell here."

So, more than fifty years later, what follows is the story of Malcolm Dingwall Mackay and his contribution to and his love for football.

It is a life based on service to the game of football and is predicated on the Club motto 'Ludere Causa Ludendi' or in other words, 'to play for the sake of playing'.

This book is dedicated to

Malky, his Family and 'The Beautiful Game'

Acknowledgements

An army of people came to our aid in the writing of this book. None was a conscript – everyone involved freely volunteered their services. When each person was invited to contribute, two things happened. Number one – a huge smile appeared on their face and, number two, they enquired – 'How can I help?' Such was their enthusiasm and eagerness to be a part of the story. Without the contributions and efforts of all those involved, this book would have remained but a dream.

The co-authors offer their sincere thanks and appreciation to:

Derek Allan, advisor; **Tam Brodie**, friend; **Richie Brown**, Darwin Creative Media; **Peter Buchanan**, QPFC; **Kirstie Couzens**, Castle Vale Publishers Ltd; **Sean Davenport**, QPFC; **Zoe Diompy**, ACF Sports Promotions Ltd; **Matt Edwards**, friend; **Graeme Elliot**, J C Roxburgh (Insurance Brokers) Ltd; **Sir Alex Ferguson**; **Niall Harding**, West Coast Traincare Ltd; **Jim Hastie**, QPFC;

ACKNOWLEDGEMENTS

Lord William Haughey; **David Hunter**, QPFC; **Alan Irvine**, QPFC; **Kings Park Hotel Management and Staff**; **Tom Lucas**, friend; **The Mackay Family**; **Ian Maxwell**, Scottish FA; **Keith McAllister**, Queen's Park Supporters' Association; **Andy McGlennan**, QPFC; **Liz Mills**, City Facilities Management Holdings Ltd; **Jim Nicholson**, QPFC; **Ann Quinn**, Scottish FA; **John Reilly**, friend; **Eric J Riley**, Celtic FC; **Andy Roxburgh**, Former Scotland Manager; **Graeme Shields**, QPFC; **Paul Smith**, advisor; **Raymond Sparkes**, ProStar Management Ltd; **Craig Stewart**, Media Associate; **John Taylor**, QPFC.

Foreword

By Sir Alex Ferguson

Going back all those years to my time at Queen's Park, Malky Mackay was a young player there and was training with the youth team. As the records show, his history at Queen's Park produced well over 300 appearances as a player and he also proudly represented his country 20 times as an amateur.

His enthusiasm for Queen's Park was easily recognised and his eternal love for his club was unmistakeable. After a fantastic playing career he was honoured to be installed as President of Queen's Park, a fitting tribute to a true Queen's Park legend and a good man.

May 2024

Chapter One

'Out O' The East There Came A Big Man'...

You could excuse Malky's parents, George and Charlotte, for being more concerned than usual following his birth in 1942. Both of them knew of friends and family who had relatives involved in a World War.

Every able male over sixteen years of age and under forty-two years of age was liable to be 'called up' to serve the country.

Malky's Dad was exempt due to his engineering background and he continued working in his employment during the war years at Hillington, Glasgow – a far cry from his native Dingwall. He was an enthusiastic Rangers supporter as were his brothers.

Glasgow, which was home to the family has often been described as a 'football-mad city'. That is a fair assessment considering it hosted Celtic, Rangers, Clyde, Partick Thistle, Third Lanark and Queen's Park. It is also worthy of note that at the turn of the 20th Century, and only some thirty years or so after Queen's Park kicked off this whole football thing, Glasgow had three of the biggest stadia in the world – Hampden, Ibrox and Parkhead.

Clyde had just recently triumphed in winning the Scottish Cup in 1939, defeating Motherwell 4-0 in front of 94,000 vociferous and passionate fans at the national stadium, Hampden Park. The cleaning staff at Shawfield Park would have the task of keeping the trophy polished and safe until eight years later when Aberdeen returned victorious northwards after defeating Hibernian 2-1. The beaten team contained Scotland legends, Willie Ormond and Eddie Turnbull.

The name of Queen's Park FC had already been inscribed on the trophy on ten occasions prior to this.

Unlike the 1914-1918 war, all senior football was cancelled. Food shortages became widespread and a nation had to learn to adapt to austerity and uncertainty. Hunter Davies, the esteemed author and football fan, managed to capture the mood of a nation in a title of one of his books.

'The Co-op's got Bananas' may not resonate much with the current population of Great Britain but for those reared on turnip and mash this news that fruit was available is the football equivalent of a headline screaming out – 'Scotland score in added-on time to win the World Cup... and England go home as runners-up'.

Those players who survived National Service resumed playing afterwards and allowed Malky's Dad to see his beloved Rangers FC.

Malky started his primary school career at St Brigid's, not far from the family home in Baillieston, a working-class suburb in the east of Glasgow.

Glasgow's reputation in shipbuilding meant that, like other British cities, it would be subjected to aerial attacks from the German Air Force, that is, when the Luftwaffe got fed up trying to destroy London after seventy-four successive nights of bombing.

In Glasgow the locals got used to the new concept of a 'bomb site'. This was usually a tenement building or commercial premises which was unlucky enough to take a direct hit from above. The authorities moved quickly to raze it to the ground for fear of further potential injury to nearby residents. Glasgow was densely populated at this time. Except for its notable public parks there was little scope for outdoor recreation.

Street football thrived; but now there was a difference.

The newly created 'gap sites' meant there was space for jackets and jumpers to be laid on the rubble and football to be played. The war effort meant that most lamp posts had been removed for use in converting to military equipment but the few that were left gave the players a kind of floodlit football.

At the age of ten, Malky was already immersed in the football culture serving as a ball boy at Celtic Park.

Malky did well in his school examinations and graduated to Our Lady's High School in Motherwell.

This establishment holds an honoured place in the history of Scottish football. Admittedly, it was some time after Matt Busby had been educated there, but Malky did share the premises with two other pupils who achieved football immortality and against whom he would compete frequently during their careers – Billy McNeill and Bobby Murdoch. These two pupils both became established international players and were part of the Celtic team which won the European Cup in 1967.

So what was it about this school that made it special? "Well, they had some really good people in the sport section. Most of them had been trained at Jordanhill College – and they had been well trained. Add to that a school ethos of promoting fitness and encouraging students across many sports," said Malky.

"I was given tennis coaching as well," he continued "And I really liked it too."

With a school-leaving age set at fifteen years, many youngsters left to pursue apprenticeships and combined that with football careers. For the most talented among this group, the popular route was signing a contract with a Junior Professional football club, either on amateur or professional terms.

Scouts patrolled the youth leagues to try and spot the cream of the talent. There was a hierarchy among the adults who attended schools' football, the juvenile leagues and particularly the Junior Professional leagues. Many of the chief scouts had themselves been professional players and the 'behind-the-scenes work' that they carried out could result in spotting the next big player. Take the following for example:

> Billy McNeill was signed by Blantyre Victoria, Bobby Murdoch played for the 'Wee Rangers' namely Cambuslang Rangers and before them Matt Busby could be seen in a Denny Hibernian strip.

During our research for this story we learned of one amateur player in the early 1960s being visited at home by a scout who offered him a contract with a senior club and a lucrative fee for signing on. The youngster had received rave notices and several clubs were keen to recruit him. At that point he was an amateur player and not contracted to any team. This meant he could move freely where he chose and no transfer fee would attach. The scout offered him a signing fee of £3,000, but the lad's father thought that other clubs in the queue would be more generous, and so he advised the boy to take some time to think about it.

The scout patiently explained what his club had in mind to maximise his potential but didn't push his offer. Eventually the scout asked the boy did he need to think about it a bit longer at which point the youngster replied, "No thank you, I don't need any more time, what I do need is a loan of your pen to sign the contract."

The player went on to have a long and distinguished career, including playing for Scotland.

In today's terms the signing-on fee he received was worth about £55,000.

In contrast, Malky said "I was really enjoying my football at Coltness United. I already had a job at Philcote, a factory run by the Scottish Co-operative where I was learning office duties. So although I was playing for a Junior team I did not earn any money, as I signed a contract remaining as an amateur player. The Junior league was hard and there were a lot of tough guys around, but I was tall and able to look after myself. I played inside-left position, which in these days was No 10, and I was rarely injured. I also had good health. It was at this time that the call came from Queen's Park in November, 1961."

Most of Malky's playing career at Queen's Park took place in the 1960s.

In that ten-year period Scottish teams achieved an astonishing record of success, reaching at least the quarter finals of European competitions on nineteen occasions.

Whilst Rangers and Celtic dominated that list, Dundee, Kilmarnock, Dunfermline Athletic and Hibernian also contributed to raise the nation's football profile. 1967 stands apart from all the other years in the history of Scottish Football. First, Celtic became the first British team to be Champions of Europe by defeating Inter Milan in Lisbon by two goals to one.

Tommy Gemmell, Malky's former team mate at Coltness United, scored the first of Celtic's goals in that game. Earlier in the same season Celtic and Queen's Park played each other in the quarter-final of the domestic cup competition, the Scottish Cup at Parkhead.

On that March day after twenty-eight seconds of the game Malky shot towards goal and saw the ball deflected into the Celtic net by a home-team player, Tommy 'Big Tam' Gemmell. Celtic went on to win that game 5-3 and lifted the trophy shortly after that.

The Celtic players who triumphed in Portugal were anointed as 'Lisbon Lions'.

Malky says, "We were all part of the Glasgow football community and although Queen's weren't in the top league we often came up against the Glasgow clubs in cup games, friendly games and even behind-closed-doors, pre-season warm ups. There were also many social events that we shared as well."

The second reason for 1967 being so memorable is that Rangers just failed to defeat Bayern Munich, losing 0-1 after extra time in the other main European Competition of that era, the European Cup-Winners' Cup, in the final game in Nuremberg, then part of West Germany.

That two Scottish teams, less than six miles apart, from the same city achieved such success is truly remarkable.

But at Wembley in April the success story continued as Scotland defeated England 3-2 with seven of the Scottish starting-eleven coming from Celtic and Rangers. Big Tam was selected for that game, but left it to his team mate, Bobby

Lennox, to score the second goal.

One other Glasgow-born player must have had to build an extension to his home to accommodate his trophies and medals. Ronnie Simpson had returned to end his career at Celtic Park after winning two FA cups with Newcastle United. The 'Queensparker' triumphed with his trademark modesty at both Lisbon and Wembley. *Note – the term 'Queensparker' denotes being a member of the Club Association for former players, coaches and staff.*

Malky wasn't unique in combining work with the demands of playing top-class football. There were other amateur players who juggled the same work/play relationship and relied upon employers acting favourably for time off. So, if Queen's drew Forfar away in the Scottish Cup on a mid-week fixture then his request might be met with 'Aye ok, but bring back a couple of bridies for the tea-break'.

So what was in it for the employers? "Well, they always regarded it as good publicity that an employee was in the public gaze, given the popularity of football in the Scottish mind-set. My employer, British Engine, was part of a world-wide insurance group. I was always supported by British Engine as they never let me down whenever I needed them," said Malky.

There was also the issue of part-time professional players who operated the same work/play combination. One of the most famous of them, Ian McMillan, had an interesting situation in the spring of 1961 as his football employers, Glasgow Rangers, became the first British team to reach a European competition final.

McMillan, who wore the Scotland strip on six occasions, better known as the 'Wee Prime Minister', was a mining surveyor when he was not bamboozling opposition players with his sublime skill. 'Ah, McMillan I see you have put in for time off next week for this Fiorentina game. That will be ok, but can you check out this water ingress report at Shettleston pit before you go? And, the wife really likes a bottle of Italian wine'.

Malky would also receive international recognition as his career progressed and represent Great Britain in attempting to qualify for the Olympic Games of 1968.

***

Here's that 'Big Man'

Chapter Two
5, 4, 3, 2, 1

In 1964 Manfred Mann released the song 5, 4, 3, 2, 1 which reached No5 in the UK Singles Chart and launched the group into stardom. It was adopted as the signature theme tune for the ITV pop music television programme *Ready Steady Go*. However, two years before, in 1962, QPFC launched Malky on the unsuspecting cohort of Scottish football league teams at the tender age of nineteen. He scored all four goals in his first appearance for the First XI in a 4-4 draw with Queen of the South. 'Follow that,' they said. So he did, scoring three in his second appearance against East Fife at Methil. He went on to score two in his third game against Dumbarton and one in his fifth against Brechin City, 5 (games) 4, 3, 2, 1 (goals). One could forgive the team selectors for thinking to themselves – Aye, *Ready Steady Go*. Malky the Mann had arrived at around the same time as the group and both were smash hits.

When Colin Stein signed for Rangers from Hibs in 1968 and scored eight goals in his first three games, many people thought that this was a record for a newly signed player. Sorry Colin, you were six years too late!

So the die was cast. Malky went on to make 433 league and non-league appearances from season 1962/63 to season 1975/76 and scored 163 goals along the way. He holds the position of second highest scorer in all competitive games in the Club's history, twenty-nine behind Mutt McAlpine (1919 to 1934) and six ahead of his erstwhile contemporary Peter Buchanan. His last First XI appearance was in January 1976 when he was a second-half substitute in a 2-2 draw with Cowdenbeath at Central Park, although it should be noted that he was still kicking people in the Caledonian League on behalf of the Hampden XI in the late 1980s.

Malky had left Coltness United and signed for QPFC, having been spotted by a teacher who was a friend of his father. In November 1961 he had been scouted by Messrs Omand and Tyson from QPFC – a photograph of the Scouting Report (plus transcription), along with a letter from the Ground Secretary of QPFC inviting him to turn out for his first game for the Reserves against Stenhousemuir, can be found at the end of this chapter. Queen's were lucky to sign him because, as can be seen from the Scouting Report, there was considerable interest from other clubs. Celtic, Nottingham Forest, Newcastle and Motherwell are recorded as wanting to trial and/or sign him. Rangers were also targeting him but withdrew from the competition for their own reasons. He also had direct approaches from Airdrie and Albion Rovers.

So, like many before and after him, he passed through the 'Hampden Gateway'. We have termed it thus, simply because the Club was recognised as the breeding ground for so many aspiring young footballers, many of whom went on to greater things as players, coaches, managers and as individuals. A large part of the culture at QPFC was not only coaching youngsters to become artisans of their chosen sport, but equally to instil in them virtues of honesty, integrity and sportsmanship.

Queensparker Alan Irvine (Player – QPFC, Everton, Crystal Palace, Dundee Utd, Blackburn Rovers; Manager – Preston North End, Sheffield Wednesday, West Bromwich Albion, Norwich-Interim; Assistant Manager – West Ham) had this to say in his letter of support for Malky's MBE award in 2015:

"I joined QPFC as a fifteen year old in 1973. Although he was still playing at that time, he took time to make young players like me feel very welcome and comfortable at the Club. He was my first coach and I have no doubt that his enthusiasm, passion, integrity and knowledge played a huge part in shaping me as a footballer and, more importantly, as a person. I have worked with many top managers and coaches during my years in professional football, but none have been more committed or

dedicated than Malky, who has voluntarily given up his spare time to help others for many, many years. I consider myself very fortunate to have worked with someone like Malky. He was a fantastic role model for a young boy like me. He was inspirational. He taught me things which helped me to become a professional footballer, but he also taught me important values such as honesty, respect, trust, humility and fairness. He has been a wonderful ambassador for QPFC and has been a huge influence on countless boys like me. His selfless efforts over the years, for no personal gain, deserve to be recognised."

The list of other Queensparkers who have made it through the 'Gateway' is not unimpressive. It includes but is not limited to:

> Sir Alex Ferguson; Ronnie Simpson; Derek Parlane; Andy Robertson; Malky Mackay Jnr; Aiden McGeady; Simon Donnelly; Steven Saunders; Paul McGinn; Bobby Clark; Blair Spittal; Lawrence Shankland et al.

Make no mistake, some didn't make it and the 'Gateway' was not a one-way turnstile to success and, notwithstanding QPFC's amateur status, the bar was set quite high. If you weren't good enough you exited by the same means as you entered, with a 'Cheerio' that went something like 'Thanks for coming but don't give up your daytime job yet son'.

In light of his auspicious start, Malky was asked if he felt like he could almost walk on water at the Club but, in his characteristic unassuming and modest way, he pointed out that, "Yes, it was a good start, but at the same time it denied some of the other young players a chance of playing for the First XI and I was acutely aware of that."

Training was hard, taking place three evenings a week and, for most, getting to and from Hampden was by public transport – all in a day's work. When Malky signed, there were four teams – the First XI; the Reserves; the Hampden XI and the Under-18s – so competition for a place was high. Let's remember that none of the playing staff was remunerated in any way, shape or form and, contrary to some reports, there was no such thing as 'boot money'. The old stories about a ten shilling note being left in a player's boot if he'd had a good game are exactly that – stories. The only recompense any of the players got was their travelling expenses incurred in getting to and from training sessions and games. Like Malky, most of the players had daytime jobs and families and so fitting in training and games was no mean feat.

Getting to Hampden from Baillieston was not easy. It involved things called tramcars, buses, trains and shoe leather – and the same on the way back. We invited Alan Irvine to provide us with an expert view on how training had changed over the years and he had this to tell us:

"As a player I don't remember being coached as players are today. In those days we did training sessions rather than coaching sessions and you learned about the game from comments by the manager and his staff, senior players and your own experiences, both good and bad, in training sessions and games.

As an example, when I first signed for Everton from Queen's Park, the manager, Howard Kendall, was still registered as a player and he would sometimes play in reserve games. I can honestly say that Howard coached me more in those games than he ever did as a manager.

I also received "in game" coaching from senior players in training games and matches. When I played my first reserve game for Everton, I played alongside senior players who were recognised first team and international players. These players had played hundreds of first team matches and they took it upon themselves to help the young players throughout the match, no doubt in the way that older players had helped them when they were young.

This "in game" coaching was invaluable and it is a shame that young players are no longer exposed to this. However whilst it taught you about your role in the team and your positioning in and out of possession, it didn't help you with your own, individual development. This was something you had to figure out for yourself.

In the past the manager told you what to do and you tried to do it without asking questions. Nowadays you explain why you want players to do things. You have to sell your ideas to them and persuade and convince them that this is beneficial for the team and for them as individuals.

Most sessions nowadays are coaching, not training sessions, even if this is disguised within the session. A lot of time is spent planning and evaluating sessions whereas in the past many sessions were clearly off the cuff. Players now expect to walk onto the training ground and see the whole session set up.

Players also expect detailed information about the opposition as a team and individually. As a player I was often told that I needed to work out the strengths and weaknesses of my direct opponent in the early stages of the game. Technology and the huge increase in analysis, means that players have all of that information well in advance. Players also expect a game plan, and a plan B, for every match. This was never available in the past.

The support team around players, on and off the pitch is now enormous, which is certainly a huge improvement from the days of a manager, a trainer and a 'sponge man'. However the down side of all of this support is that we have created coach dependent players and a lack of leaders. This is something which needs to be improved."

Getting into the First XI was not a 'given' when papers were signed. At that time, and before the advent of a Women's squad, there would be fifty to sixty players on the books, all vying for a place in the top team. The standard operating procedure was to be watched early on in the training sessions and the Coach then determining when a player should start and in what position. Malky didn't hang about getting picked for the First XI.

Malky's daytime job was working for an engineering insurance company called British Engine, which was based in St Vincent Street in Glasgow's city centre. British Engine was owned by Royal Insurance for whom a certain Cammy Thomson worked – and played with Malky at QPFC between 1970 and 1977. Malky was well liked by everyone in the organisation and made his way up through the ranks to a senior management position. He was respected by his colleagues and customers alike. Combining his business acumen with his schoolboy sense of humour made him good fun to be around.

Whilst he was forging his career and playing for QPFC, the management team was very supportive in allowing him leave of absence to go touring with QPFC and Middlesex Wanderers. Undoubtedly though, and as discussed in the previous Chapter, it certainly did the profile of the organisation no harm in having a top-flight footballer as an employee and the same could be said for the Royal

THE QUEEN'S PARK FOOTBALL CLUB, LTD.

Scouting Report – Season 1961/62.

Game: Coltness United v Thorniewood United

Date of Game: 25th November 1961

Player	Position	Team
Malcolm Mackay.	I.L.	Coltness United.

I attended the above game accompanied by Mr. Tyson but unfortunately Mackay was not playing.

He and three other players were 'rested' because of the Scottish Cup Tie versus Stonehaven – at Stonehaven – on Saturday 2nd December.

We made ourselves known to the officials of Coltness United – a very cooperative set of officials – and they introduced us to Mr. Mackay, who is a fine upstanding lad of nineteen years of age and when I asked him if he would like to play for Queen's Park he beamed and said 'I would love to.'

My information is he will be allowed to play a trial as soon as his club is out of the Scottish Cup.

The following teams want to sign or give him a trial – Celtic, Notts Forest, Newcastle, Motherwell.

Signature: Wm Omand

Date: 27/11/61

Transcript of Scouting Report, November 1961

The Queen's Park Football Club, Limited.

Founded 9th July, 1867.
TELEPHONE: LANGSIDE 1275.
TELEGRAPHIC ADDRESS:
SPIDER, GLASGOW.

JAMES LOGAN, C.A.
SECRETARY.
J. GILLIES,
GROUND SECRETARY

HAMPDEN PARK,
MOUNT FLORIDA,
GLASGOW, S.2

JG/EG.

6th March, 1962.

PERSONAL.

M. Mackay, Esq.,
112, Swinton Crescent,
BAILLIESTON.

Dear Malcolm,

You will no doubt be aware of the fact that I wrote your Club Secretary, Mr. J. Rhinds, on Wednesday last, 28th March, 1962, requesting permission to play you in the Strollers XI -v- Stenhousemuir F.C. game on Saturday, 10th March, 1962.

I wired yesterday requesting advice from him, and asking him to telephone me, which he did later in the day, acknowledging that my letter had been received, but as he had other two players involved on the day in question, stated that he would put my request before his Committee last evening.

This morning, Mr. Rhinds telephoned me to say that my request had been granted, accordingly, I shall be glad if you will turn out in this game, and to that end, I show hereunder the team arrangements.

Mr. A. West, Secretary of the Strollers XI will be delighted to welcome you, and the friend whom I understand will accompany you, as Mr. Rhinds himself will not be able to attend on this occasion.

I trust that you will have a good game, and shall look forward to hearing the report, and meeting you later.

Yours faithfully,

Jas. Gillies.   Ground Secretary.

Arrangements Reference.

Fixture	:	Strollers XI -v- Stenhousemuir F.C.
Venue	:	New Lesser Hampden Park.
Date	:	10th March, 1962.
K.O.	:	3 p.m.
Attend	:	Not later than 2.30 p.m.
Dinner	:	A.F. Reid & Sons Ltd., Gordon St., Glasgow, after game.

Malky's letter from the Ground Secretary at QPFC

Don't let the smile fool you!

Harry Davis's instruction was easy to understand and act upon as far as Malky was concerned 'Just keep on doing what you do best, upsetting defenders and scoring goals.' Harry had succeeded Malky's first coach, taking over from former Hibernian 'Famous Five' legend Eddie Turnbull in 1965.

In Chapter 1 we introduced Malky against the context of life in Scotland during the Second World War. In the mid-1960s we were informed that austerity had passed and 'We never had it so good'.

"Well, Mr Auld, in these circumstances I would be obliged to insert your name in my little black book and dismiss you from the field," Tiny answered.

"Mmmm....., well, what if I just THOUGHT that you were a useless B****** but didn't say so?" Bertie asked inquisitively.

"Ah, that would be perfectly acceptable with no disciplinary action justified," Tiny continued.

"Well, in that case, I just THINK you are a useless B******!" Bertie joked.

In those days, football was a game full of characters. Bertie and Tiny certainly fitted the bill! There was a certain rapport and respect between the officials and players which sadly appears to be missing in today's modern game.

***

'unruffled' could have been created for him. As the clock ticked to the final whistle Malky collided, nay, lunged into an opponent in a desperate attempt to win the ball. With the stricken defender crying for his mammy, Tiny trotted over to the scene, organised first-aid for the bewildered defender then turned his attention to the offender.

Malky was sure he would be in the bath earlier than the others as the opposing fans chanted the usual "OФФ, OФФ, OФФ."

Tiny's right hand slid into the pocket which contained the notebook. "Ah, Mr Mackay, just checking the time-piece. Not long to go now before we can all go off together. Kindly behave yourself for the short time that is left," he smiled.

Malky dodged the bullet.

The late Bertie Auld also left us a great story about Tiny's sense of humour which never deserted him even in the midst of torrid Rangers v Celtic battles.

Bertie Auld was a more than competent football player. He fancied himself as a referee as well and this day during a break in play, entertained Tiny in a manner we feel sure he would have appreciated.

The bold Bertie shouted "Haw, ref, if I said you were a useless B****** would I be in trouble?"

in the winter of 1968 attracted 134,000. In these days football was a truly working man's passion after a hard week of work.

We are not talking all-seater stadia here, either!

Unlike now with kick-off times running from midday until eight-thirty in the evening, Saturday games were all scheduled for three o'clock in the afternoon. Midweek fixtures usually started at seven-thirty in the evening with Wednesday the regular day. Special trains were put on for travelling fans with departure times set for delivering supporters in time for the kick-off and waiting for the final whistle before returning.

We asked Malky about referees "Aye – they are all part of the game – you just had to get on with them," he said.

Mr Tom Wharton, known as Tiny Wharton, was one of the best known whistlers during the 1960s. He was taller than Malky and twice as wide; Tiny was prominent in training aspiring referees across Europe and also in football's governing body FIFA.

The authorities liked him to handle the hard games – so that would make him equally unpopular with Rangers and Celtic fans, they thought. There was a humorous occasion in which the name of Malcolm Mackay was already printed in the referee's notebook for a foul tackle; Tiny never raced around the pitch, ambling was more his style. The word

However, for huge numbers of fans who worked in hourly-paid occupations, Saturday morning working was essential to put enough notes in something called a wage packet – and even better if they could get Tuesday and Thursday night shifts as well. All over the United Kingdom newspapers with sports pages were essential reading for fans and print workers' shifts were fixed around kick-off times. There were even special Football Editions printed in a variety of coloured paper, green and pink in particular. Many a time a young son would be sent to the local newsagent at six o'clock on a Saturday evening to wait for the delivery of the paper giving the Saturday scores. The Dads could then catch up on all the scores, stories from the games and league tables and check their football pools coupons!

By the end of Harry's own playing career he had played in the European Cup Winners Cup final of 1961 – unfortunately Fiorentina prevented Rangers from being the first British team to win a cup in the liberated continent.

When Jock Stein managed Dunfermline Athletic in the Scottish Cup Final in 1961 at Hampden, 113,618 fans turned up to witness it. After that 0-0 draw, 87,866 fans returned to see the Cup head to Fife four days later. There were many remarkable attendances. For example in February 1968 Elgin City played Arbroath in front of 12,608 fans; Clydebank v Hibernian drew 14,900 witnesses and Scotland v England

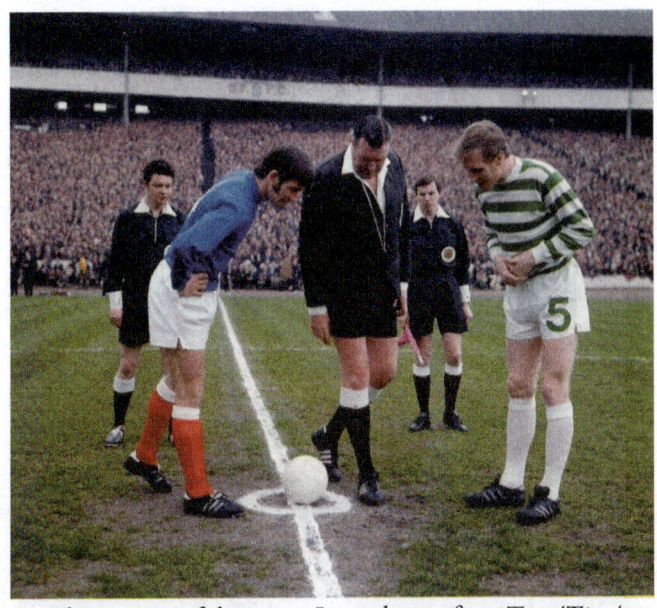

Three giants of the game: Legendary referee Tom 'Tiny' Wharton checks out the result of the coin toss with Old Firm captains John Greig and Billy McNeill before the 1971 Scottish Cup Final. In the background, Hampden's North Stand and Terracing is jam-packed.

Chapter Four
The Wanderer(s)

So, continuing the musical theme, no, this Chapter does not relate to that Status Quo hit which reached No7 in the UK Chart in 1984. Nor does it refer to Malky's predilection for sauntering around his opponents' penalty areas at will, but rather his affiliation with the highly respected invitational football club, Middlesex Wanderers Association Football Club (The Wanderers). He toured not only with them, but also with the Scotland Amateur International squad, QPFC, and, oh yes – the work's team.

The Titanic sank in 1912, the same year as The Wanderers Club was launched, and thankfully, it remains afloat today.

The Wanderers started life as Richmond Town Wanderers in 1905, having been established by brothers Bob and Horace Alaway following the collapse of a team named Richmond Town Association Football Club, with which the brothers had been associated and which also sank... due to financial difficulties after taking part in a costly and unsuccessful tour of France back in 1901.

The specific purpose of the new Club was to perform 'missionary work' in Europe where football was still in its relative infancy. Initially, success was achieved through using local amateur players and, anxious to make one more tour, the team made a short trip to Calais in 1906. This proved to be a huge success and as a result more invitations followed. As the years progressed and the fixture list continued to grow it was clear that there was a need to field stronger teams and so, in 1912 it aligned itself to Middlesex County Football Association and adopted the name Middlesex Wanderers. The Club's constitution set out its remit as:

- to promote a good fellowship among football clubs and other sporting organisations throughout the world

- to send teams of British footballers on tours abroad

- to play occasional football games in the British Isles and such other games as the Executive may approve

In order to compete with the improving standard, the scope of selection was widened to include players of amateur international standard from the four Home Nations and a close link was established with Queen's Park FC. Queen's

Park players started touring with The Wanderers in 1953 and it proved a successful liaison. Probably the most ambitious of the Wanderers tours was that which took place in 1967 to the Far East and involved playing in six different countries.

The Wanderers have toured Japan and South Korea a handful of times – the first being in 1967. Malky played in the 1969 tour along with three fellow Queensparkers – Pat Hamill, Alex Sheridan and Derek Stewart. They played six games over a twelve-day period with the spoils being almost equal. Malky had (and still has) a fear of flying – unless it was into an opponent's ribcage – so it was no mean feat for him to make the tour. Harry Davis suffered the same phobia so maybe they 'coached' each other through the long-hauls.

The Wanderers and QPFC shared the same amateur status and ethos of spreading the football 'gospel' and their visits were warmly welcomed by the authorities of the hosting countries. One astonishing outcome of their pilgrimages was that games were played in front of huge crowds which any league club would be proud of today. By local standards, and bearing in mind that the majority of the spectators had never seen a football match before, the spectator numbers were almost unbelievably high – 20,000 to 30,000 was a 'normal' gate.

Two years later in 1971, Queen's players John Taylor, Tommy Barr and John McLaughlin went with The Wanderers on another tour of Japan and one of the games was played in Akita in the north of the island. No foreign team had ever played there and the crowd number was also in the tens of thousands. Bearing in mind that the population of Akita is 316,000 today, and allowing for the usual population growth trends, it meant that somewhere near 25% of the entire town's inhabitants turned out for the spectacle. One thing that still puzzles John Taylor to this day is how 5,000 Japanese fans behind his goal knew his name was Jimmy!

The Wanderers Club has toured Japan on eight occasions, the most recent being in May 2005 and is synonymous with touring. It has completed over one hundred tours to forty-four countries since its foundation.

In the spirit of fellowship shared by both Clubs, they decided to play against each other. The Wanderers visited Hampden in May 1989 and the game ended in a 2-2 draw – a fitting result.

A concluding tale on The Wanderers relates back to the Carling Cup final of 2012 which is covered later in Chapter 6. Co-author Dave was at Wembley with Malky for the game and after a meal in the stadium they went for a 'wander' around the facilities and to stretch the legs. Ambling past hundreds of others doing the same, a voice shouts out "Hey Malky, how are you?" We meet with the gentleman and pleasantries are exchanged. Dave asks Malky, "How do you know that chap?"

"Well I toured with him at Middlesex Wanderers," was the reply. So, out of a crowd of 89,041 and 400 miles from Baillieston, we bump into someone who knows Malky! Such is the popularity of the man.

In the same year as Denis Law was helping team-mates Bobby Lennox and Jim McCalliog defeat the newly crowned 1966 World Cup Champions at Wembley in 1967 in front of 99,063 fans, Malky was hammering in goals for the Scottish Amateur International side. Also against England, at a slightly smaller ground (Tannadice), he scored both goals in a 2-2 draw in front of a crowd of 800 – yes, eight hundred!

In August 1926 the Scottish Amateur National team had been formed and the Scottish Amateur Football Association announced that the first Scotland amateur international match would take place against their English counterparts.

So, on 18th December that year at Filbert Street (the home of Leicester City FC) and in front of a crowd of 10,000, Scotland Amateurs beat England 4-1. For this match the team selection was determined by the Scottish FA.

Malky represented Scotland no fewer than on twenty occasions over a five-year period between 1966 and 1971, scoring six goals. This places him sixth on the list of all-time appearances and joint-fourth on the list of most goals – just one goal behind Peter Lorimer! He also represented Great Britain in a game against Sweden U23s in Gothenburg in 1967.

Playing for the national side was a huge highlight of Malky's football career and in his own words he commented, "Aye, it was an honour to be picked to represent your country but I treated every game the same, no matter who the opposition or what the competition, I just played for the sake of playing – and, oh aye, to win." One of the international competitions Malky recalls excitedly was the 1967 UEFA Nations Amateur Cup. Scotland reached the final in Palma de Mallorca having beaten Spain in the semi-final in front of 20,000 fans at the Luis Sitjar Stadium on 16th June. Two days later they faced Austria in the final at the same stadium but lost 2-1 in a closely fought game.

Scotland may have lost the game but the players and officials had not lost their sense of humour. All but two of the team comprised Queen's players and the team coach was QPFC's own coach – Harry Davis. After the team had lost to Austria, Harry told the boys that they would not be leaving Palma until three o'clock in the afternoon the following day so they could go down to the beach in the morning and enjoy themselves – which they did. All hotel rooms had to be vacated by ten o'clock in the morning so the players put their belongings in a communal area in the hotel lobby. When they returned to put their suits on, it was clear that the clothes had all been mixed up so that they looked like a bunch of misfits and had no time to sort themselves out before the team bus left for the airport. It is rumoured that the QPFC Committee Members who had travelled with the Squad had repaid the boys for some earlier misdemeanours in which Malky – it is alleged – had played a key part!

The team played its final match on 5th April 1974, a 1-1 British Amateur Championship draw with England at Highfield Road. The team ceased to exist later that year, when the English FA abolished the distinction between amateurism and professionalism in domestic football.

Mentioning 'The Lawman' and Malky in the earlier paragraph is no coincidence and it brings to mind another interesting wee story. To mark the stadium's 100th birthday, QPFC held a centenary dinner at Hampden. Co-author Dave was privileged to be one of Malky's guests and Denis was there too! Dave managed to catch up with The Lawman and reminded him of an event at a petrol station in Bowden, just south of Altrincham. It was a Saturday in 2003 and Dave was returning home after an overnight stay in Dunham Massey and, having refuelled, was waiting patiently in the kiosk to pay. Looking out the kiosk window, he saw a top-of-the-range Jaguar briskly halt at one of the pumps and the driver hurriedly proceed to put in what looked like a fiver's worth of petrol – in a Jag?? Dave thought the driver looked remarkably like Denis Law. It was. The Lawman rushed past those waiting in the queue with a, "Sorry boys and girls – I'm doing a TV commentary at Old Trafford and I'm late – see you," and sped off.

Denis amazingly remembered the event and apologised again, with one of those characteristic huge grins on his face. At that point he said, "Excuse me, but I just have to dash and grab an autograph."

"Whose?" Dave enquired.

"Well, Malky's of course," was the response. And he did.

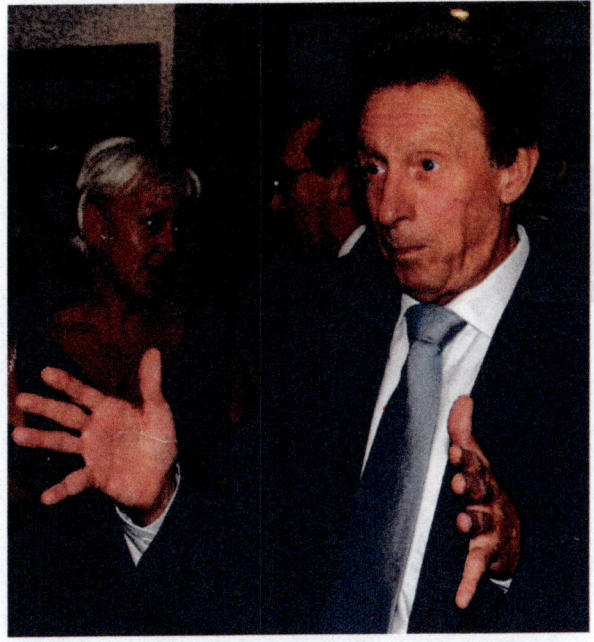

Denis the 'autograph hunter' at the Centenary Dinner

There were many tours with QPFC but John Taylor recalls one which stands out – Nigeria in 1965. On a day off, two of the Nigerian officials took some of the players to the main market in Lagos, under strict instruction never to pay the asking price and secondly, to go in groups of four or five. Malky, John and Charlie Gilmour went together and Charlie sold his old watch, which was on its last legs, to a market trader for the equivalent of £2. On returning to the team coach, a fellow player, Alex Ingram, proudly showed off a watch he had just bought for £3. Charlie asked to see it, prodded it and it burst into a thousand pieces, at which point Charlie told Alex that he had just bought his old watch! Malky was found not guilty of any involvement in this malarkey, if you believe that!

There will be a wide range of opinion on the causal effect of these tours on the development of football in African and Far Eastern countries. Some of the facts speak for themselves. In addition to the star players in Malky's native east end of Glasgow team, Celtic, and across teams in Scotland and England generally, a quick European scan reveals South Korean and Japanese players at Bayern Munich, Paris Saint-Germain, Feyenoord and Royale Union Saint-Gilloise.

The ultimate answer may be provided when, or if, one of these nations lifts the World Cup itself. Ach well, if Scotland doesn't achieve it we will share a wee tad in their glory!

And last but not least – the work's team. Yes, Malky managed to cram in these demanding trips as well as all the others outlined above. Some games were quite local but others were in far-flung places like Cardonald! King George V playing fields, known affectionately as the 50 pitches, were visited regularly in matches for the Mark Hurl trophy, which was the insurance equivalent of the Champions League. That said, in the good old days when employers organised and funded sports & social clubs for the benefit of staff, British Engine benefited from the facilities provided by its parent company – Royal Insurance.

The Royal had a brilliant sports complex called Bardhill in London and Malky, aided by Queensparker, Cammy Thomson, led the Royal Glasgow to turn out as UK branch winners in the 1972/73 season. At that time, co-author Alan played in the Royal Insurance Group's London team and Dave was in the Malky team but fate did not have it that they played against each other. Who knows how that would have ended up?

***

The Royal/British Engine cup-winning team 1972. Standing left to right: A Fraser, G Dunn, W Logan, A Crawford, J Cook, J Muir, A Gilchrist, C Thomson. Seated left to right: A Robin, D Stewart (co-author), M Edwards, A Thom, M Mackay

Chapter Five

'The First Cut is the Deepest'

On 21st May 1999 a match took place at Hampden between a Queen's Park Former Players side and a Celebrity All Stars team. The purpose? To commemorate the official re-opening of Hampden Park following major reconstruction of the South Stand.

At this point it's worth remembering that the current Hampden is Number 3. The first one has its origins in a transaction which took place in 1857 when Glasgow Corporation bought the Pathhead estate which comprised Queen's Park itself, the Queen's Park Recreation Grounds – affectionately termed 'The Recs' – and some sheep grazing land now known as Myrtle Park. This was the Club's first ground and the fields were acquired on a short-term lease of seven months for the sum of £20. The ground was christened Hampden Park in recognition of the recently constructed row of houses high up on the ridge known as Hampden Terrace.

However, the intervention of a planned Cathcart Circle Railway Line some twenty-six years later meant that the Club's expansion plans would be restricted by this slightly inconvenient infrastructure development and so another site was needed. Hampden Number 2 was only a few hundred yards away to the north-east but rapid expansion meant that they outgrew that too and yet another site was sought – but where?

On the other side of Hampden Terrace a 12.5 acre site was purchased in 1900 for £10,000 – hello Hampden Number 3. The site the Club left became home to another legendary Scottish footballing team – Third Lanark and they renamed it Cathkin Park.

Many decades later and during the late 1970s, it became apparent that the facilities at Hampden were in need of renewal.

The first phase of the redevelopment involved the demolition of the North Stand, the concreting of all terraces and the building of a block of turnstiles around the upper section of the East Terrace. This work began in October 1981 and was completed in 1986, reducing the capacity from 81,000 to 74,370 and costing £3 million. A second phase had been planned to begin in 1988, but the release of the Taylor Report after the Hillsborough Disaster, in which ninety-seven men, women and children died – and 766 were injured – caused the plans to be redrawn and the proposed costs escalated to £25 million.

In 1992, the UK Government provided a grant of £3.5 million which allowed work to begin on a £12 million project to convert Hampden into an all-seater stadium. The last match played in front of the sloping terraces was the 1992 League Cup Final, Hibernian 2-Dunfermline 0. Within a year, the east and north parts of the ground had been converted from terracing to seats, and the partially rebuilt Hampden was re-opened for a friendly match between Scotland and the Netherlands on 23rd March 1994. It was then also used for the later stages of the 1993-94 Scottish Cup competition. As the capacity of the old South Stand had been limited to 4,500, the total capacity of Hampden had been reduced to approximately 37,000.

The final stage of the renovation began in November 1997, at a cost of £59 million – funded by the National Lottery and by early 1999 the works had been completed. The pressure was on to demonstrate that the ground was 'fit for purpose' and that safety certificates had been issued in order for the 'Old Firm' 1999 Scottish Cup Final to proceed on the 29th May 1999. The new and current capacity is 51,866 – a far cry from the record of 183,724 which prevailed in 1937!

So Malky, along with his buddies at QPFC, came up with the idea of hosting a Former Players v Celebrity All Stars match. One can only imagine the enormity of the task ahead – no, not the game itself – but rather proving the efficacy of the structure, corridors, lounges, hospitality suites, cloakrooms, escapes, fire protection, communication systems, crowd control, policing, stewards, PA systems, lux levels, parking... and the list goes on. It's worth remembering that the ground needed to host a target number of high-profile games in order to manage the financial side of things, so this was a key event.

Malky has variously been described as 'fearless on the park and fearless in the boardroom' and never have truer words been spoken. He was never aggressive nor assertive in this regard and is probably best described as 'slightly more than mildly persuasive!' John Taylor manages a huge grin when he recounts that the mere mention of Malky's name in the boardrooms of Scottish league teams up and down the land always raises smiles.

Anyway, undaunted, he picked up the phone to Rod Stewart (Sir Rod was just 'Rod' back then but it wouldn't have mattered anyhow), Kenny Dalglish and Ally MacLeod, amongst others. Ally was asked to manage the QPFC team and is recorded in the official match programme as saying "My wife, Fay, and I were delighted to receive Malcolm Mackay's invitation to attend and to be involved in what I'm sure will be a night to remember." It was on Fay's birthday as well.

'THE FIRST CUT IS THE DEEPEST'

Managing the Celebs was down to none other than Rangers legend Alex Miller.

Before the match, Ally commented that his opposite number would have a game on his hands. He said, "I am sure that the Queensparkers put at my disposal will be up to the challenge. Alex has many stars but he doesn't have Dixie Ingram, Eddie Hunter, Alan Irvine, John McGregor, Bobby Dickson, Austin Reilly, Jimmy Nicholson or Malky Mackay," to name but a few.

In reply, Alex cautioned, "Some of my players will think of this as a light-hearted occasion, however there are others for whom the first blow of the referee's whistle will ignite their competitive natures. Guys like Gordon Strachan, David Hay, Kenny Dalglish, Graeme Souness and Willie Miller don't play friendlies. I've got a couple of aces up my sleeve in Jim Kerr and Rod Stewart, who are both accomplished players, but I will be assuring my boys that they can't take it too easy. I can well remember from my Rangers days that pre-season friendlies against the Spiders were amongst the toughest matches of the entire season to play in. In fact, looking back, I'm only too glad that I'm not having to face the likes of Dixie Ingram or Eddie Hunter tonight."

It is worth spending a few pounds on the official match programme which is available online – it is a terrific read and lists the players in each squad. When commenting on

Malky, it goes like this, "Malcolm Mackay – he has turned minimisation into an art form and, whilst others run about silly to score goals, he will use the least amount of energy possible to achieve the same result. Hey, isn't that the sign of an extremely clever and skilful player?" Yes Sir, indeed.

In the pre-match euphoria, Malky was asked to pen a few words of wisdom. Under the title of 'A Festival of Football' he wrote:

"It was only whilst in discussion with the Editor a week ago I came to realise that, perhaps subconsciously, tonight's main event owes its origin to my own playing days in the Sixties. Nowadays it is accepted, and rightly so, that many of our best young players will eventually leave to join better teams. That was not always the case.

Queen's Park's constitution does not allow players to retain their membership of the Club should they decide to turn professional but, in my time, it was almost as if there was a stigma attaching to former players and they appeared to be socially ostracised by those who had spent their entire playing careers at Hampden. It seemed strange to me that I should build up relationships over the years with various players and yet, just because they chose to improve their standard of living by playing football elsewhere, overnight my attitude towards them was supposed to be different. In my mind they were still my friends and there was no 'great divide'.

Nowadays, of course, former professionals are welcomed to the Club provided that they are prepared to adhere to our traditions and play for the Club as amateurs – that is to say – not receiving one penny (other than travelling expenses) for their efforts. Sadly, that change in attitude has come too late for those players representing Queen's Park this evening but tonight's match provides them with the opportunity to wear the famous black and white hooped jerseys one more time and to mix with stalwarts like Dougie Grant, Eddie and David Hunter, Jim Nicholson, Austin Reilly and myself who chose to remain and were glad to do so.

Ironically, it is thanks to another former player and friend, Alex Ferguson, that we have this opportunity. Had Manchester United not enjoyed such success at all levels of their Club this season, thereby forcing them to cancel their intended fixture with us, then tonight's match may have remained an unfulfilled dream."

And so say all of us, Malky.

Anyway, back to the title of this Chapter and hats off to Alex Miller for his timely caution to his team before kick-off. With the game progressing nicely, if not too 'friendly', Eddie proceeded in 'Eddie style' to give some attention to Rod. The picture at the end of the Chapter provides a flavour – watching on in the background are Jim Hastie and Tommy Burns.

When Rod released the song in 1977 it stayed at No1 in the UK charts for four weeks and the second line of the song goes, "But there's someone who's torn it apart." The slight collision between Eddie's boot and Rod's leg resulted in an unplanned visit to the treatment room for Rod, whereupon the duty doctor could have been forgiven for saying to Rod, "*So this is the first cut and it's quite deepish.*" Anyhow, he proceeded to stitch the wound and send Rod back on! Maybe Rod had a premonition way back then but, in fairness, he was singing about his heart, not his leg. How appropriate were Alex's warnings before the game? After the match, Rod filed a complaint to the authorities – no, not about the tackle, but rather that there were no hair dryers in the changing rooms! The authorities duly fitted the said articles in all changing facilities. Nice one, Sir Rod!

Rod was back at Hampden on 3rd July1999, this time to concentrate on the 'day job' with the opening concert of the new Hampden.

So, the match went without incident, ignoring the event just described, and the ground was officially deemed 'fit for purpose' and given a FIFA 5-Star rating. The positives are obvious – the Old Firm Cup Final did take place and just for the record, Rangers ran out victors 1-0 in a closely contested game – but 30,000 fans paid for tickets and programmes for the Celebs game which produced valuable revenue for all those involved.

'THE FIRST CUT IS THE DEEPEST' 61

It really was a 'Festival of Football'.

"Ouch!"

Chapter Six

The Palaces

The Honours system of the United Kingdom has a long history, with the appointment of Knights Bachelor dating back to the Norman Conquest in 1066. Not to be outdone by this, in 1687 King James VII of Scotland and James II of England founded the Order of the Thistle to reward Scottish nationals for their service. Queen Anne increased the number of knights from eight to twelve and in 1827 the number was further increased to sixteen, which is the current number. The only foreigner admitted to the Order has been King Olaf V of Norway.

Moving the clock forward almost two-and-a-half centuries, King George V created the Order of the British Empire in 1917 to honour those who had served non-combatant roles during the First World War. The outbreak of the War and the sacrifices made in all areas of society had led to a desire to widen the Honours system.

This was also the first time women were honoured on such a wide scale throughout all levels of the Order.

So, the Order was twenty-five years old when Malky was born. The Honours system celebrates people who go above and beyond to change the world around them for the better. The system recognises the people who have:

- selflessly volunteered their time and efforts
- gained the respect of their peers
- displayed moral and physical courage
- showed real innovation and entrepreneurship

Sir Winston Churchill summarised the Honours system with his innate sagacity – "The object of giving medals, stars and ribbons is to give pride and pleasure to those who deserved them."

Remaining apolitical and accepting that there are people in the United Kingdom who neither recognise nor support the system, and that is absolutely their prerogative, there are those who agree with Sir Winston. Supporters would argue that there are literally tens of thousands of awards which have been bestowed upon people from all backgrounds and across all sections of communities for a myriad of just and good reasons.

Co-author Dave had been contemplating for some time nominating Malky for an award in recognition of his love for and selfless contribution to football. So, early in 2011, with the encouragement and support of his family and a couple of close friends, he decided to start the 'awards journey'.

The protocol is relatively straightforward and there is excellent online guidance covering the whole process from start to finish. It is not a short exercise and a successful nomination will take, on average, anything up to two years from the date of submission to go through the validation of the claims in the nomination and its worthiness. This will vary depending on the activity involved and how much information is in the nomination papers. Dave was living and working in London at the time and as fate would have it, London was hosting a wee affair called the 2012 Olympics. It was pointed out in dialogue with the Cabinet Office that things therefore 'might be a little busy'.

Completing the form was easy – the hardest part was what to leave out. Malky had made an outstanding contribution to the sporting youth in Scotland by dedicating himself to the development and nurturing of aspiring young footballers. His selfless drive and determination had focused on young sportsmen from all parts of the country, acting as coach, mentor and role model to all comers, including some who were perhaps less fortunate than others.

THE PALACES

One of 18th Century English poet and author William Blake's famous quotations is 'the road of excess leads to the palace of wisdom'. Malky certainly had the wisdom but never did anything to excess – except perhaps training. He has never smoked, been a drinker (other than his usual tipple of Irn Bru) and has always looked after himself physically and mentally. A testament to his physical condition is displayed by the photograph shown below.

Malky in his prime

His voluntary dedication and devotion to the development of young players and his appetite for seeing youngsters flourish as artisans of their sport and as individuals was awesome. His dogged determination to help others knew no bounds.

Malky is a trustworthy individual and was sought out by the Scottish FA to represent the Association on tours with youngsters in the UK and Ireland. The purpose of those tours was not only to enhance the playing skills of his charges, but also to further their own personal development and broaden their horizons as individuals.

He is a modest man and seeks no self-aggrandisement from his efforts and, if anything, spurns praise. There are many, many good and right-minded people involved in football but what set Malky apart was the sheer determination, passion and zeal with which he set about his tasks, for absolutely no self-reward.

One of the key requirements of the nomination process is to have the nomination supported by no less than two letters of support. Letters can be from:

- senior persons from the candidate's organisation or community

- high profile members of the community e.g. MPs/Councillors

- persons who regularly work with the candidate

and the letters must:

- confirm that the candidate is doing or has done what they are being nominated for

- confirm that an honour would be supported by the community

- include significant, recent achievements

- describe the impact that the candidate has had

So, the Nomination Form duly completed, this part of the procedure commenced by enlisting the aid of Malky Mackay Junior (MMJ). At the start of the process MMJ was manager at Watford, having taken over from Brendan Rodgers in June 2009.

In June 2011 he had left Watford and taken the helm at Cardiff City. In his first season at Leckwith Road he guided Cardiff to their first ever League Cup Final in 2012. His opponents? – Liverpool, managed by none other than a fellow ex-Celtic legend – Kenny Dalglish. Cardiff had booked their place in the final by squeezing past Crystal Palace in a penalty shoot-out and the following day Liverpool dismissed Manchester City to reach the final. MMJ tells us that he had just finished some TV work at the Liverpool game and as he was leaving Anfield his phone beeped. It was Kenny who had sent a text saying "See you at Wembley for a cup of tea."

The Final took place at Wembley on Sunday 26th February 2012 and MMJ is recorded as having said that leading his team out on to the pitch for a cup final at Wembley alongside Kenny Dalglish doing the same was the zenith of his career. A crowd of 89,041 watched a gripping cup final which saw Liverpool lift the Carling Cup, after winning 3-2 on penalties following a 2-2 draw at the end of extra time.

Kenny and MMJ had met before. One of their more memorable meetings was back in 2009 when MMJ was on a UEFA Pro-Licence course, sitting in a lecture room with other managerial hopefuls. "We had people talk to us," recalls MMJ. "Some lectured and some did Power Point presentations. Then it was Kenny. He just appeared with a mug of tea – fifteen of us round him – and said, 'Right boys, fire away.' It was a question-and-answer session and two and a half hours later we were still there. He told some great stories and there were some absolute pearls of advice. It was one of the most valuable two and a half hours of my professional life and I will never forget it."

At the start of the 'awards journey' the 'Gaffer's office' at Watford's training ground at London Colney was the venue for MMJ to host a series of meetings, during which he would validate the historical data gathered on his father, add valuable material to that data and facilitate a letter of support from

Sir Alex Ferguson. Care was exercised at these meetings, as confidentiality is a key requirement of the Honours process and at no point must the nominee be aware that he or she is under consideration.

Through the good offices of MMJ and the late Lyn Laffin (Sir Alex's PA for over thirty years) Sir Alex's letter was turned around in short order. A copy of his letter and two others are shown at the end of this Chapter. Malky and Sir Alex have been life-long friends and MMJ has a great relationship with Sir Alex also, who had agreed the loan of Tom Cleverley from Old Trafford to Vicarage Road at this juncture in the process.

Contemporaneous with this, Dave met with Alan Irvine up at Everton's Finch Farm training ground. In similar fashion, Alan had no hesitation whatsoever in writing his letter of support. The final letter of support came from the late George Smith CBE, who was Dave's manager and friend at the British Engine in Newcastle and held Malky in high esteem.

So, with all the paperwork done it was time to submit the nomination. The Honours and Appointments Secretariat within the Cabinet Office was at that time located in Admiralty Arch, London. Rather than risk the submission containing these precious original letters going astray in the post, the nomination was hand-delivered. A staff member took the file and cautioned against any feeling of rejection if nothing was heard for about two years, perhaps even longer, given the Olympics.

And so the clock ticked for what seemed an interminable period of time. Doubts began to creep in but MMJ, in his inimitable supportive fashion, was full of praise to all those involved in the initiative even if it turned out to be unsuccessful.

On a fairly uneventful day in October 2014, Dave was at home on annual leave. The telephone rang. The call was from a PPI recovery firm offering a no-win, no-fee service for a loan which never existed. The call was terminated. Thirty minutes later, another call was received from a no-win, no-fee firm of ambulance-chaser lawyers for an accident which never happened. This call, too, was terminated. And yet again the phone rang. The conversation went something like this:

D – "And what do you want?"

The caller asked, "Is that Mr Dave Stewart."

D – "Yes."

Caller – "I am calling from the Honours and Appointments Secretariat at the Scottish Parliament. May I speak with you?"

D – "Of course and please forgive my manner. I have just received two time-waster calls."

Caller – "I understand. Now, have you nominated a Malcolm Dingwall Mackay for an award?"

D – "Yes."

Caller – "Good. I have to tell you that awards are not made posthumously so can you confirm that Mr Mackay is still alive?"

D – "Well I spoke to him last week and have not had any bad news since then so I guess 'yes' is the answer, but mind you he is so laid back that at work we used to wake him up from time to time to check for a pulse."

Caller – "And are you aware of any criminal offences having been made against him since the submission of your nomination?"

D – "To the best of my knowledge – absolutely not."

Caller – "Thank you, Mr Stewart."

D – "May I read anything into this conversation?"

Caller – "Thanks again Mr Stewart and Good-day."

Quite a morning! A few weeks later an official-looking letter from the Scottish Parliament arrives at Malky's house. His wife calls him at work and he laughs it off but suggests she opens it. The letter is from the Honours and Appointments Secretariat stating that he is to be offered the award of

M.B.E. (no, not Manager at the British Engine!) – but rather 'Member of the Most Excellent Order of the British Empire' **'for services to football in Glasgow'** and would he be minded to accept it? Malky jokes that it must be a wind-up. Unconvinced, his wife calls MMJ who says "Mum, it's no wind-up and I've known about it for three years."

Malky duly accepted the award with grace. This led to yet another road to a palace, only this time it was the Palace of Holyroodhouse where the Investiture took place. He received his medal from the late Queen Elizabeth II in the presence of a small family gathering. Mrs Mackay had pleaded with Malky not to dare mention the 'Hampden' word to the Queen in the same way he does to nearly everyone he ever meets. Yep – you've guessed it. The 'Hampden' word was heard crossing Malky's lips and, under interrogation, he admitted to asking Her Majesty if she had enjoyed the 2014 Commonwealth Games which, of course, Hampden hosted. Her Majesty smiled and replied "Yes, very much thank you."

***

THE PALACES

A happy day at the Palace of Holyroodhouse

So Malky joins MBE ranks with some of Scotland's finest footballing legends. The list features many well-known names, including Billy McNeill, Danny McGrain, Frank McLintock, Ally McCoist, Willie Miller, Andy Robertson... and the list goes on. At the time of the award Malky was, and remains, the only Queen's Park Football Club amateur player or official to have received a Queen's Award. As well as being a distinguishing mark of the individual, it is a worthy credential of the Club and its motto – 'Ludere Causa Ludendi' or, in other words, 'to play for the sake of playing'.

If one studies the list, a fairly rudimentary fact which emerges is that the only amateur player to appear on that list is Malky. Few begrudge footballers a decent and comfortable standard of living, bearing in mind that the career of a professional footballer can be a short one and halted at any time through injury. Their earnings however, which could sometimes equate to the GDP of a small country, present a stark contrast to Malky's seven and a tanner, paid three times a week for tramcar and bus fares to and from Mount Florida. For our younger readers, seven and a tanner today will buy you a third of a packet of crisps.

At the Queen's Park Football Club Annual Dinner at Hampden on 6th November 2015, the second speech on the Programme was 'Tribute and Presentation to Malcolm D Mackay M.B.E' by Councillor Archie Graham, Glasgow City Council. Rapturous applause followed and a wee tear in either eye could be seen on Malky's face.

***

THE PALACES

QPFC 2015 Annual Dinner Programme

In conclusion, it should be noted that there is a clear expectation that those who have received an honour are, and will continue to be, role models.

Where the recipient of an honour has brought the Honours system into disrepute, honours can be cancelled on the advice of the Honours Forfeiture Committee and with the approval of The Sovereign.

Behave yersel, Malky!

WHAT 'AM SAYIN' TO YOU IS...

AF/LL

17 January 2012

Cabinet Office
Honours and Appointments secretariat
Ground floor
Admiralty Arch
London
SW1A 2WH

Dear Sirs

Re: Malky McKay

I am recommending the above named to be included in the Queens Honours List. I do so with the knowledge and friendship of over 50 years.

He decided to play as an amateur for Queens Park Football Club, instead of playing professionally. As you may be aware Queens Park is a complete Amateur Football Club and the lure of money would never change that.

In his almost 50 years at Queens Park he went through all the various positions in the Club as Player, Coach, Team Manager, Committee member and President with the utmost sincerity, honesty, integrity and enthusiasm. These qualities are always admired and applauded not only by his friends and colleagues but from all sections of the football family in Scotland, he is unquestionably a rare and special human being.

Thank you for taking the time to consider this request as I'd go with total belief that Malky McKay deserves to be honoured for his services to his country.

Yours faithfully

[signature]

Sir Alex Ferguson CBE

MANCHESTER UNITED FOOTBALL CLUB LIMITED
Trafford Training Centre, Birch Road off Isherwood Road, Carrington, Manchester M31 4BH
Telephone: 0161 868 8700. Facsimile: 0161 868 8855. www.manutd.com
Registered in England No. 95489. VAT No. GB 561 0952 51
Registered office: Sir Matt Busby Way, Old Trafford, Manchester M16 0RA

Sir Alex Ferguson's MBE support letter

THE PALACES

16th December 2011

Cabinet Office
Honours and Appointments Secretariat
Ground Floor
Admiralty Arch
London
SW1A 2WH

Dear Sirs

I have known Malky McKay since I joined Queens' Park FC as a fifteen year old schoolboy in 1973. Although he was still playing at that time, he took time to make young players like me feel very welcome and comfortable at the Club.

He was my first coach and I have no doubt that his enthusiasm, passion, integrity and knowledge played a huge part in shaping me as a footballer and, more importantly, as a person. I have worked with many top managers and coaches during my years in professional football, but none have been more committed or dedicated than Malky, who has voluntarily given up his spare time to help others for many, many years.

I consider myself very fortunate to have worked with someone like Malky. He was a fantastic role model for a young boy like me. He was inspirational. He taught me things which helped me to become a professional footballer, but he also taught me important values such as honesty, respect, trust, humility and fairness.

He has been a wonderful ambassador for Queens' Park FC and has been a huge influence on countless boys like me. His selfless efforts over the years, for no personal gain deserve to be recognised at this time.

Yours faithfully

ALAN IRVINE
Academy Director

Alan Irvine's MBE support letter

BDS DEVELOPMENTS (NORTHERN) LTD
DIRECTORS: GEORGE SMITH CBE, DON BURN

5 KENSINGTON COURT
SOUTH SHIELDS NE33 3DT
Tel: 0191 456 6971 (M) 0785 585 2746

24 January 2012

Dear Sirs

I would like to support the nomination of Malky Mackay for a UK honour. I have not known him as long as Sir Alex Ferguson but I agree with all he says about him. He was a colleague with me when we worked with the British Engine Insurance PLC

He has devoted his life to amateur football, to the Queens Park Football Club and to the Hampden Park Club. He has been a player and manager of the team; he has been a leading member of the club Committee for over thirty years and was their President.

Malky has had many opportunities to go to larger clubs, where there are substantial rewards but he preferred to serve football in a voluntary capacity. Over the years he has been an inspiration to the hundreds of young players some of whom some became professional players but all have benefited by playing for the club under the leadership of Malky. By his example they have learned self-discipline, team work and leadership skills which has benefited them for the rest of their lives.

He is a man of the highest integrity, his contribution and commitment to youth football over such a long period has been outstanding and is an example to others.

Yours sincerely

[signature]

georgesmithcbe@yahoo.co.uk

Honours & Appointment Secretariat
Cabinet Office
Admiralty Arch
London SW1A 2WH

George Smith's CBE MBE support letter

Chapter Seven

'Extra Time'

So, as this story approaches the final whistle it's time for reflection. We've looked at Malky's achievements and contributions to his Club, his Country and to the footballing communities in Scotland, the rest of the UK, Ireland – and indeed the world at large in the form of touring with QPFC and The Wanderers. There have been many good and loyal players, Members and staff who have served the Club, but what sets him apart from the crowd is the longevity of his association with Queen's Park Football Club.

We also take time out to have a look at some of the funnier moments in a long and varied career – the hardest part being what to leave out.

At the end of the 1972/3 season Malky had stopped playing in the Queen's Park first team, but continued to represent the Club in its Hampden Eleven for several years. It was during this period that he played centre-forward in a reserve league match with Malky Junior playing centre-half as the team were a man short. We asked him what it was like to play in a league game in the same team as his son. "Yes, we did play one league game together for the Reserves. I was up-front despite the fact that I was fifty. There was never any rivalry between us, we are not like that," he remarked. One wonders if any other father/son duo, perhaps the Messrs Lampards or Redknapps, achieved a similar feat?

MMS and MMJ

At the same time, and in his assumed role of coach and mentor to younger players, he would voluntarily take time out to offer advice to any of the youngsters who had been approached to sign professional forms by other clubs.

The 'apprentices' were on one-year contracts when they signed for QPFC so many of them were targeted by the bigger clubs at quite a young age. Much in the same tradition as the likes of Bill Shankly and Sir Alex Ferguson, Malky would focus on the issues which may – or may not – be in the youngsters' best interests. These would include the views of the parents, the proposed club location, reputation, owner, manager, pay, lodgings, and the like. One of his key recommendations was for the player to go and train with the proposed club over a few sessions and see if the individual felt it was the right move for him. What many people do not know is that Malky would often give up his time to go and train with the youngster too and offer up his opinion.

He served the Club as Match Secretary for the Club's minor elevens and also was a member of the General Committee of Queen's, eventually holding the position as Club President from 1993 until 1996.

This era of his service to the Club off the pitch is notable for his vital contribution to the redevelopment of Hampden Park as described in Chapter 5. The project fell in and out of the public gaze for years while other candidates were promoted as genuine rivals to become the National Stadium. Murrayfield, the home of Scottish Rugby, was put forward for consideration along with Celtic Park and Ibrox Park.

Local and national politicians became involved and the issue was rarely out of the news. Malky was at the forefront of the project to retain Hampden as a national resource and he tirelessly took part in the protracted planning process. This was the 'Malky reinvented' period of his distinguished career and featured his 'fearless in the boardroom' credentials. 'Talk is cheap and time is expensive' characterised his approach.

He also played 'up-front' in the redevelopment of Hampden and its transformation into a concert venue and to hosting the 2012 Olympic football fixtures as well as the 2014 Commonwealth Games. All through the processes Malky was at the heart of things, tirelessly providing information for the decision makers and utilising his business skills honed during his career in commerce. He also served as a Scottish Football Association Committee Member and on the Glasgow Football Association.

Malky eventually stood down from active committee work in 2020 at the age of seventy-eight, nearly sixty years after he signed on from Coltness United.

All through these years and to this day, he still attends home and away fixtures in the company of other ex-players.

Over this astonishing period of his football career, Malky has retained his schoolboy sense of humour which is still in perfect working order. A few memorable stories spring to mind:

The Match-Maker

He assisted a friend who was between jobs with setting up an interview. Hosting the meeting was Ms X, a senior vice-president of the organisation. Opening remarks exchanged, Ms X proceeded to advise the interviewee that she had enjoyed a long and prosperous business relationship with Malky and that, "He is the only man in this City I allow to call me 'Hen'."

The Cardonald Orange

At half-time in one of those 'Champions League' matches at Cardonald, one of the players headed towards a colleague on the touchline who had brought some oranges. "And where do you think you're going," blasts Malky from the centre circle. "To get an orange," was the reply. ***What 'am sayin' to you is...*** you've naw played anywhere near well enough to peel the bxxxxy oranges never mind eat one, so get yur posterior back here!" Or words to that effect.

The Paisley Snowball

Just before kick-off at a match against St Mirren, it started snowing. Malky proceeded to start a snowball fight with the opposition – no details are recorded of the result. What *is* documented is that the referee glared at Malky, but instead of calling him over for an entry in his wee black book, he called the match off.

'Over the Sea to Skive'

Warming up on Gayfield Park (which is always a good idea, given its proximity to the North Sea) before a game against Arbroath, Malky wondered if he could whack the ball out of the Ground, over the promenade and into the sea. He did. The match ball is probably still commuting between the little Danish town of Skive on the Jutland peninsula and Arbroath. The latitude of Skive is within 0.01 degrees to that of Arbroath's so one could argue that the ball 'Ju(s)tland-ed' there!

The Pep Talk

No, this has nothing to do with the boss at Manchester City – far from it. Co-author Dave recalls another vital insurance game where, admittedly, he was not having his usual David Beckham-style first-half and was not looking forward to the team talk at half-time. He was right. Senor Guardiola would have put his arm round the individual and given some words of guidance and encouragement. In contrast, Malky's counselling was, "When you get the ball, just haud it until Ah get there," – that was the guidance – "But what you lack in ability you make up for in effort," – that was the encouragement. It worked, Dave played a blinder in the second-half and scored twice.

Play in any Position

We briefly spoke about Cammy Thomson in Chapter 2. He was probably one of the nicest guys ever to grace a football pitch and was really liked by everyone who knew, worked and played with him. Cammy was a surveyor in the Fire Dept of Royal Insurance and became great friends with Malky, who was in the Engineering Dept. Many people thought that Malky should have been in the Aerodynamics Dept because he just seemed to float around the place. Cammy joined QPFC in 1970 from the successful amateur side, City Chambers AFC and in his seven years at Hampden, rose to captain the First Team and become one of the most influential Spiders of that period.

One particular story which perhaps speaks volumes for his all-round contribution, took place during a Scottish Cup tie at Hampden in December, 1973. In the game there was consternation in the ranks when the then Queen's Park goalkeeper, Ronnie Lowrie, was sent off in the first-half following an incident with an opponent in the penalty area and with the score still 0-0.

Lowrie left the field after divesting himself of his goalkeeper's jersey which was taken by captain, Cammy, whose first task was to face the resultant penalty kick. Cammy dived to his right to finger-tip the well-taken penalty past the post, and thereafter performed various other heroics to prevent the opposition scoring. Queen's Park crept through to the next round by a narrow 1-0 margin.

Little did he realise that day that two rounds later the Club would be drawn against Rangers at Ibrox and although the end result was an 8-0 defeat, the fixture ensured that the Queen's Park Treasurer was a much happier man that evening as a result of the weighty cheque for the Club's share of the gate receipts.

Perhaps Cammy should have retained the goalkeeping position at Ibrox rather than donning his normal No 5 shirt.

So this leads to a different tale but on a similar theme. In yet another of these insurance 'Champions League' games, co-author Dave was due to play in his usual No 8 jersey but on discovering that the other team was a man short, Malky told him to change his top and play for the other side. All protestations were ignored. Not long into the first-half Dave rose for a ball and got some elbow treatment on the way up. After the event, the opponent fell to the ground and was given a wee stud on the arm by Dave in retaliation when, to his horror, he looked down to see Cammy looking up with a smile on his face that could light up Hampden saying, "Davy, tell me you didn't mean that."

"No, sorry – I forgot I was playing for them," was the timid reply. Playing in any position is one thing but playing for the opposition is quite another. Thanks, Malky!

The Final Whistle

We talked about 'Malky reinvented' above but did you know that as well as 'inventing' Malky, QPFC introduced to the sport: half-time, crossbars, free kicks, the passing game and turnstiles? The Club also fielded all eleven players in the first recognised international between Scotland and England in 1872 which was an honourable 0-0 draw.

In writing this book and before we 'left the field' we asked Malky to nominate what would be his best ever Scotland team. It reads:

Jimmy Cowan

Danny McGrain   Billy McNeill   Davie Provan

Graeme Souness   Willie Fernie

Jimmy Johnstone   Kenny Dalglish   Denis Law   Willie Johnston

Alan Gilzean

We wonder if Andy Roxburgh would agree with his team selection?

We hope that you've enjoyed this epic journey as much as we have. It is a poignant fact that it all started with seven Speysiders kicking a ball around Queen's Park Recs 157 years ago and we have them to thank for 'The Beautiful Game'.

That venue also happens to be where the authors of this book played their last game together in the heady heights of the Glasgow Menswear Sunday League. Co-author Alan scored the winner in a 3-2 victory with a beautiful right-foot volley from an inch-perfect pass (oops, an assist) from his wee brother.

And finally, should Andy Robertson, the captain of Scotland, whose career was refreshed by Queen's Park, lead the team out at the opening game of Euro 2024 in Germany this summer, Malky will be kicking every ball – just like the rest of us!

***

Chapter Eight

'...To See Oursels As Ithers See Us'

We were assisted by many people in the production of Malky's story and here is what some had to say about him...

Peter Buchanan, ex-fellow player:

"Yes, our plan was to get right stuck in; Malky was 'harem scarem' and we relied on two wingers to set us up with goals. I was right footed but best with my heading and Malky was lethal with his left foot. The tactics were simple – score goals.

Eddie Turnbull and Harry Davis were major influences on me; yes, I had many offers to turn professional but was happy to stay with QPFC – my dad played for them as well – and I had a good job with Belling Cookers, then with the Famous Grouse. We had some right good parties in the coach's house which was then very near the ground.

I share Malky's assessment of Billy McNeill; I played against him many times in cup competitions and he never kicked me once. An absolute gentleman."

Andy Roxburgh, Former Scotland Team Manager:

"The Spider with the Big Heart.

Malky Mackay Snr and I first met in the early sixties when we both joined Queen's Park FC as teenagers. The Club was amateur back then, and with the demands of work and football, the Club's motto 'To play for the sake of playing' was a core requirement. Malky was the epitome of the wholehearted, passionate footballer – a goal scorer with a commitment to the Club that money couldn't buy.

Over the years, I watched from a distance as he dedicated himself to the black and white hoops (more than 350 appearances). He consistently found the net during his great career and caps for Scotland Amateurs and Great Britain recognised his praiseworthy performances at club level.

After giving his all on the pitch, he dedicated himself to the Club's development as a committee member and then as the President.

And, it was no surprise when, in his seventies, he received the MBE for his services to football. This has been a lifetime of loyalty to one club and a total commitment to the Club motto.

As the head of a footballing family (his son Malky Jnr became a top pro player and an elite coach), Malky Mackay Snr has proved one thing: he carries the ball close to his heart and consequently, his passion for the game is infectious."

Lord William Haughey:

"My association with Queen's Park goes back over 52 years, starting as a boy playing for Queen's Park in the under 16's and up to the present day being a sponsor of the Club, the one constant over this period has been 'Mr. Queen's Park, Malky Mackay'.

Every football club should have someone like Malky in its midst, his passion for Queen's Park Football Club is immeasurable, for over five decades he has served in many roles with distinction.

Over the last two decades I have worked closer with Malky through the Glasgow Cup, he has single handedly battled to maintain the significance of this wonderful trophy. His knowledge and guidance have been of great assistance to me, it is fair to say that my continued support and sponsorship of the Glasgow Cup is testimony to Malky's gentle persuasion.

It is fitting that there will now be a book that will record Malky Mackay's wonderful contribution."

Ian Maxwell, Chief Executive, Scottish FA:

"Malky truly is a stalwart of Scottish football. When I was a young player at Queen's Park, he was always around to offer advice and I remember him playing the odd game for the Hampden XI when he was in his fifties. He's been a regular friendly face at Hampden, either through his QP roles or those within the various committees and board he has served on with the Scottish FA, SPFL or SFL. He won't admit it himself, but he's played a key role in the development of the Scottish game and has the utmost respect of all those who have come across him, on or off the pitch."

Raymond Sparkes, ProStar Management Ltd., Advisor to M Mackay Jnr:

"For some (in a certain generation of footballing circles) the mere mention of a club and/or a surname, can often trigger an immediate link, an association – a special alignment if you like!

And so it is, that when Queen's Park FC is talked about, the name Mackay is never far from being amongst the very first names that spring to mind.

In recent times, it's been Malky (Junior) who has spearheaded the name in that part of this trail but... it is in every era prior to that, that we need to look to acknowledge Malky (Senior) as where that introduction was made and indeed cultivated into the bond that inextricably links the name Mackay to one of Britain's most iconic football clubs!

Senior – as a Former Player, Coach and President of The Spiders – is the man who forged a relationship that in only recent years, earned him the right to an MBE – a quite rare accolade, and one only ever awarded to those who have made an extraordinary contribution in their sector, in Malky's case, for services to football over 60 years!

I've known Senior for over half that period and so can testify to the above being a more than an accurate reflection of the impact he has made on the game but beyond that – and perhaps most importantly – it is as patriarch of the Mackay family at large where I know him to be at his best. It is something I've been privileged to witness first hand given my proximity to the family, in my role as a professional advisor to Junior over the period.

And so this is just to say... that as an undeniable, legendary figure at Queen's Park and indeed Scottish Football as a whole, the name Malky Mackay is established as one that not only continues to gather reverence wherever it is heard but moreover, is one that is also firmly placed in the annals of our game here in Scotland!"

Eric J Riley, Director of Celtic Football Club:

"Malcolm D Mackay, a.k.a. Malky, has not only been a wonderful servant to his beloved Queen's Park for many, many years, but also to Scottish football generally, and Glasgow football in particular.

As a player, Malcolm played over 350 games for Queen's Park in the Scottish Football league. Thereafter, he became a very influential football administrator, serving on a number of committees with the SFA, SPFL, SFL and the Glasgow FA in addition to his various roles at Queen's Park. Our paths crossed on a regular basis as I have been a Director with Celtic for almost 30 years and for almost all of that time served on many of the same committees as Malky. I recognised that I would be working with Malcolm rather than against him and we developed a close and respectful working relationship which is now a friendship.

Malcolm is friendly, likeable, personable, kind, enthusiastic, helpful, tenacious, committed, competitive, knowledgeable and an experienced individual who is always anxious to ensure individuals are encouraged and given the opportunity to play sport generally and, in particular football, with the resultant health benefits this can bring to individuals and society generally.

At the Glasgow FA he was viewed affectionately as the elder statesman, held in the highest esteem, greatly regarded and respected and often the voice of reason as he mentored the various committee members. He was also a great advocate of youth development, not only for the elite but for all youngsters.

Malcolm's network in football was superb and I'm sure such contacts resulted in him being retained in the insurance sector well beyond retirement age for the doors he could open and the business he could generate.

Malcolm had many, many fantastic experiences and a huge number of stories to tell. I was always amused when he raised with me his role as a ball boy at Celtic Park and the fact that his pay was never settled in full.

Malcolm Mackay has had a huge impact on Scottish football over many years. However, the most important aspect to his life has been and remains his family and I am sure that will not change in any shape or form.

It has been a privilege and a pleasure to have known Malcolm and to have worked so closely with him over the years."

Keith McAllister, Life-long Queen's Park Supporter:

"I have a couple of stories about Malky.

He was a real maverick; he did his own thing and was a joy to watch. Incredibly skilful with a wicked shot, I seem to remember that he always played with his shorts rolled up quite high for some reason. There were a slew of players like him at the time; guys who could change a game, but who wouldn't find too much favour with modern managers who expect players to be tracking back and involved in absolutely everything. That wasn't Malky. He was, though, a really effective tackler when he wanted to be; he was a solid, solid guy. He had a strong build and was remarkably mobile for a bigger lad. A joy to watch when he went off on one of his great runs.

He'd be on the right one minute, through the middle the next; on the left the next. So, perhaps challenging for opponents... and his team mates.

Malky started with us when there was a coach for training, but the team was picked by the Selection Committee, which was made up of directors (or 'the Committee' as it was at Queen's). However, that changed and we eventually started to appoint what was called Head Coaches, and this guy would also pick the team.

One of our first proper managers, Joe Gilroy (who had quite a bit of success with Dundee and Fulham), came along to a supporters' meeting one night and was being asked about reasons for selection of certain players and tactics, the usual stuff. He answered and then someone asked how he involved Malky in tactic talks. Gilroy replied with a smile and shrugged his shoulders. 'When I give the team the tactics for the next game, Malky just sits in the corner and reads the paper.'

There was a story that when Malky signed for Queen's, his Mum said that she'd buy him a new shirt every time he scored a goal. He played his first game away against Queen of the South in a league Cup tie on 29 September 1962. The score was 4-4 and Malky scored all four goals. His Mum bought him four new shirts. He followed that up three days later by scoring three goals in a 4-5 defeat to East Fife. Another three new shirts. Not surprisingly, he started in the next game, away to Dumbarton and he scored both goals in a 2-1 win. That was nine goals in three games and his old Mum had to buy him nine shirts. She told him that he wouldn't be getting any more new shirts and, funnily enough, he only scored one goal in the next five games.

I was at an away reserve match near the end of his playing career. Some of the locals were trying to take a rise out of him, due to his age. Then he hammered this shot in from about 30 yards to put us ahead. The locals shut up after that.

He was my first hero when I started watching the Club; I think he was everyone's hero. In times when things were a bit challenging for Queen's, you'd go along to games hoping that you'd see a bit of magic from Malky, whether it was one of his mazy runs or that rocket shot."

Niall Harding, Contract Manager and Insurance Buyer:

An appreciation of Malky Mackay, Senior

"A genuine, down-to-earth and humble interlocutor; simply unlike any other person I met in the course of corporate commercial life in the first two decades of this century.

Malky Mackay was a unique representative of the global insurance carrier he served. An authentic, gentle man, a survivor from a bygone age of human engagement and civility when I encountered him through my work in contract and risk management for a rolling stock maintainer and manufacturer. He embodied the true spirit of that clichéd adage about conversing the same with a duke or a dustman. He always spoke plainly and simply; with an unconcern for the status and position of those he was meeting, and remarkably, with a transparent lack of personal interestedness or autopiloted attachment to his company's immediate objectives. Both of which I realised were special and endearing and made him someone especially trustworthy with whom to do business.

It was from others that I heard of his distinction as a footballer. Never from his lips. A diffident, polar opposite of most of the contemporary players of his level of skill and achievement who seem all too easily prompted to sing the praises of their own God-given athletic talent.

It was pleasing to learn that his contribution to amateur football in Scotland was recognised in 2015. This jewel of commercial integrity would have equally deserved accolades for his long career in insurance: although for remaining always his own man true to his principles and his soul – in the way of the Sir Thomas More character in *A Man for All Seasons* – I suspect such acknowledgment was more sparing than Malky deserved."

John Reilly, Baillieston Buddy:

"I've been a pal of Malky's for 60 years and live close to him in Baillieston. I've watched his career closely as a player, coach, committee man and President of Queen's with quiet admiration.

I once asked him why he never turned professional when I knew offers had come into QP for his services. 'Who'd be there to help Peter Buchanan score the goals if I left?' he would joke! I knew his commitment to that club was unconditional and he had a dedication unlike anything I'd seen before to one club.

A passionate belief of his was to advocate for football coaches of all levels getting to watch the big games at Hampden. He would say, 'The only way our country will get better at football is if our coaches are given the chance to watch the best and learn.' You know he wasn't wrong!

In later years as a Past President, he would travel with me in my car to Queen's games all over Scotland. You get used to Malcolm arguing with the Sat Nav and then telling you what road to take and how to get to the away grounds even though we'd been there 10 times before! We had great times and memories I'll never forget."

Tom Lucas, Another Baillieston Buddy:

"I have known Malcolm for over 30 years. We first met in Baillieston and knowing I was an athletics coach, he asked if I would take his son Malky for speed training as he had just signed for Celtic from QP.

This was to be the start of a lifelong friendship. Following young Malky and QP were a joy. One of the things I noticed early on about Malcolm is that at every football ground we went to in Scotland, he was treated with unbelievable friendship and courtesy.

Somehow we managed to get into the club car park everywhere we went. The window would go down he'd have a laugh with the guy on the gate... and next minute we're parked next to the main doors of the stadium...!!!

I can't think of anybody who has a bad word to say about him. Travelling with him across the country to watch his beloved QP was a joy and a privilege and I will treasure all the fun and laughs we had along the way. They broke the mould with Big Malky!"

Tam Brodie, Malky Jnr's Father-in-Law:

"I've known Malky for over 25 years.

My first impression of Malky Snr was of a well-educated, serious-thinking man, with a definite hint of eccentricity thrown in. Malky is a man with a vast knowledge and passion for the game of football with a dedication to Queen's Park that is quite incredible. It didn't really surprise me when a few years ago he was awarded an MBE for voluntary services to football in Scotland.

On a personal note, my fond memories are of the many car journeys we shared when going south to watch Malky Jnr play at various English clubs. We would be in the car for 6 or 7 hours but when you are travelling with Malky, the stories, debates and banter we had made the journey seem a lot shorter. I have always said that if he ever took up fishing he would be a natural. Let me explain...

The normal order of business would be... Malky would introduce a topic and start a discussion, then cast a line on to which I would bite, take the bait and be caught, hook, line and sinker. He would proceed to reel me in, dissecting my answer with those few words that I have over the years come to dread. "But why Tam?" Needless to say, that by the time we reached our destination I ended up in total agreement with his point of view, thinking... what just happened there! Malky had just landed another fish!

Over the years, if there was any important game being played at Hampden, Malky always made sure there was a spare ticket for me. His generosity knows no bounds. I've seen it up close and personal for years. I am very fortunate to have a close dear friend as Malcolm Dingwall Mackay MBE."

Francesca Mackay, Granddaughter:

"My Grandad has passions. Football, everything Queen's Park, Knickerbocker Glory's and Irn Bru... his favourite phrase being... I'll have a glass of Scotland's National drink please! Ever since Callum and I were wee, Grandad has always loved trying to put a smile on our faces. Whether it's telling a joke or tapping one of us on the shoulder (without us knowing), he never fails to get a laugh out of a room.

'...TO SEE OURSELS AS ITHERS SEE US'   103

Although I didn't get the football training sessions in the garden that Callum had, Grandad regularly enjoys coming to my netball matches and I've loved having him on the side-lines cheering me on.

Going to the Palace of Holyroodhouse to see him with the Queen was amazing and one of the best days. He's a real inspiration to footballers and his charismatic personality lights up any room he walks into!

I'm so proud he's my Grandad."

Callum Mackay, Grandson – currently at Berwick Rangers:

"My first memories with my Grandad are probably no surprise... playing football.

I remember spending so much of my time as a wee boy constantly kicking the ball against the garage door with him. I don't think my Mum or Gran were best pleased! We would spend ages practising dribbling, different ways of kicking a football and of course, his favourite thing to help me practise – my weaker foot.

Everything he taught me and the hours listening to him talking about the game have helped me become the player I am today.

I absolutely love having him come to my games and can sense his warmth and enjoyment at watching me play. He is and always will be my number one fan.

I spent many of my summer holidays around Queen's Park with my Grandad. Every time I spoke to someone at the Club I could tell they held him in the highest regard for his service to the football club. His passion and dedication to QP and actually Scottish football is something I'm in awe of.

I was lucky to be invited to the Palace of Holyroodhouse in Edinburgh to watch him have his efforts and achievements recognised by being awarded an MBE by The Queen.

It makes me so proud to be able to call him my Grandad.

Grandad you truly are a special man."

***

About the Authors

Dave Stewart has known Malky since 1971. Straight from school, Dave joined the same insurance company as an office junior and, under Malky's tutelage, a life-long friendship and respect developed. Dave had the privilege to play in the same work's team with the Queen's Park triumvirate of Malky, the late Cammy Thomson and Alan Irvine. He doesn't recall losing a game!

Alan Stewart is a Third Lanark supporter and Scotland fan whose daughter found it necessary to check with him before setting her wedding date that there were no competing football fixtures. He is still kicking a ball around at the age of seventy-three years and is determined to retain his amateur status.

Printed in Great Britain
by Amazon